English Code 2

Grammar Book

Contents

Welcome!

1  **Watch. Answer the question.**

What two animals is Tom?

_____ .

Tom   Leo   Anna

2 **You are Leo. Look and match.**

1   I'm a rabbit. •

2   He's a cat. •

3   We're animals. •

3  **The sentences are wrong! Read and correct them. Watch to check.**

CODE CRACKER

1   Look! It's a funny game.
2   I'm a rabbit and you're a dog, Tom!
3   Look at Anna! She's a cat!
4   Milly's a horse!

Language lab 1

I'M / I AM

I will talk about how old I am using **I am** ... / **You are** ... / **He is** ...

1 Read and label the people in the photo.

Hi! I'm Toby. Look at my photo! It's Friday and it's a music lesson! That's my music teacher, Mr. Stevenson. He's great!

There are two girls in the photo. They're Katya and Sophie. They're seven. They're my friends. Fraser and Harry are in the photo. They're my friends, too. Harry is my best friend. He's seven. We're all seven! His birthday is in April and my birthday in May!

Toby

3 _____

1 _____

2 _____

I'm = I am
You're = You are
He's = He is
She's = She is
It's = It is
We're = We are
They're = They are

2 Read again. Underline 'm, 's, and 're.

3 Match the sentences with the photos.

1 We're brothers.

2 I am your new teacher.

3 She's my sister.

4 It's winter.

5 They are my grandpa and grandma.

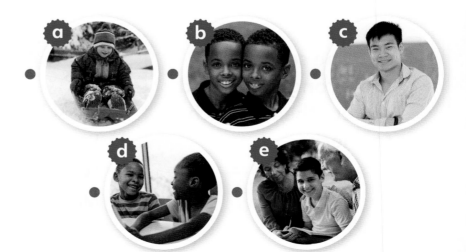

a

b

c

d

e

4 Write the sentences again.

1 It's a sunny day today! _It is a sunny day today!_____

2 They're my sisters. _____.

3 She's my best friend, Anna. _____.

4 We're eight. _____.

5 You're a good friend. _____.

5 ⚙ Read the instructions. Draw and write sentences.

1 Draw your mom or dad. Write a sentence about him/her.

This is my mom. She's great! She's ...

This is my _____ .

_____.

2 Draw two friends. Write a sentence about them.

These are my friends.

_____.

3 Draw your favorite toy. Write a sentence about it.

This is my favorite toy.

_____.

1 Out and about!

1 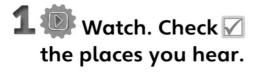 **Watch. Check ☑ the places you hear.**

1 clothes stores ☐
2 river ☐
3 castle ☐
4 bookstores ☐

2 **Read and complete. Watch to check.**

Do   doesn't like   like   likes

1 **Leo:** I _____ stores.
2 **Leo:** _____ you like stores?
3 Milly _____ stores.
4 Milly _____ cars.

🇬🇧 British
shop
🇺🇸 American
store

3 **Number the places in the order you hear them in the video. Watch to check.**

CODE CRACKER

a toy stores ☐
b bookstores ☐
c farms and parks ☐
d clothes stores ☐

Language lab 1

LIKE / DON'T LIKE

I will talk about town words using **like / don't like**.

1 Read and answer. Who likes the swimming pool?

_____ likes the swimming pool.

Dad: OK, kids. It's Saturday. Let's do something! Hmm … But what?

Sophia: Hmm … I like the farm. Do you like the farm, Will?

Will: No, I don't like farms. Sorry. I like the swimming pool.

Sophia: Sorry, I don't like the swimming pool.

Will: Oh dear … I know! Do you like the park?

Sophia: Yes, I do. Does Brutus like the park, too?

Will: Yes. He likes the park. We all like the park!

Dad: Ready, kids? Let's go!

2 Read again and underline like, don't like, and likes.

3 Look and write.

I **like** parks.

I **don't like** stores.

Does she **like** playgrounds?

Yes, she **does**. / No, she **doesn't**.

She **likes** parks.

He **doesn't like** stores.

1 I  .

I like the café.

2 He  .

_____ .

3 I  .

_____ .

4 Look at 3. Ask and answer.

Does she like the café?

Yes, she does. She likes the café.

4 He  .

_____ .

Language lab 2

THERE IS / THERE ARE

I will describe places using **there is / there are**.

1 Read. How many places are there to visit? Circle. 5 3 4

I love my city. It's Edinburgh, in Scotland. Scotland is in the United Kingdom. There are fantastic places to visit. Come and see!

There is a castle. It's Edinburgh Castle. It's very old.

There is a big park, too. It is beautiful.

There are also great museums in Edinburgh. There isn't a farm. My city is fantastic!

Is there a river?	Yes, **there is. There's** a river. 😃
Is there a park?	No, **there isn't. There isn't** a park. 🙁
Are there any houses?	Yes, **there are. There are** houses. 😃
Are there any castles?	No, **there aren't. There aren't any** castles. 🙁

2 Read again. Underline there is, there are, and there isn't.

3 Read again. Match the questions and answers about Edinburgh.

1 Is there a castle? ●
2 Is there a farm? ●
3 Are there any museums? ●
4 Are there any farms? ●

● a No, there aren't.
● b Yes, there is.
● c No, there isn't.
● d Yes, there are.

Language lab 1 and 2

1 Complete the questions and answers.

1 Is there a swimming pool?

Yes, there _____ .

2 Does she like playgrounds?

Yes, she _____ .

3 _____ there any schools?

No, there _____ .

4 _____ he like rivers?

No, he _____ .

2 Read and complete.   are   don't   is   like

Hi Jenny!

How are you? I'm on vacation! I'm in Spain with my family. It's amazing here!

There **1** _____ parks. There are playgrounds. There **2** _____ a river, too.

There isn't a castle. There isn't a museum.

I **3** _____ like museums. There is a café
and a big swimming pool! I **4** _____ the
swimming pool!

How is your vacation? Are there any swimming pools?

See you soon!

Love,

Freddie

3 Choose a picture and imagine. Make and write a postcard.

Hi! I'm on vacation. I'm in ... .

2 Day and night

1 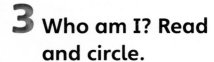 **Watch. Write the animals which sleep in trees.**

1 _____

2 _____

2 **Read and circle. Watch to check.**

1 Rabbits sleep / don't sleep in the day.

2 Porcupines sleep / don't sleep at night.

3 Bats sleep / don't sleep in trees.

4 Owls sing / don't sing at night.

3 **Who am I? Read and circle.**

CODE CRACKER

1 I sing at night.   rabbit / bat / owl

2 I sleep in the day and at night.   dog / porcupine / owl

3 I don't sleep at night.   dog / bat / cow

4 I don't sleep in a tree.   owl / bat / porcupine

Language lab 1

I GO / DON'T GO

I will talk about daily routines.

1 Read the quiz and circle for you. What's your score?

1 Do you eat apples and bananas every day?

Yes, I do. / No, I don't.

2 points / 1 point

2 Do you brush your teeth in the day and at night?

Yes, I do. / No, I don't.

2 points / 1 point

3 Do you play sports?

Yes, I do. / No, I don't.

2 points / 1 point

4 Do you sleep at night?

Yes, I do. / No, I don't.

2 points / 1 point

5 Do you wash your face in the morning?

Yes, I do. / No, I don't.

2 points / 1 point

Your score

5 – 6 Eat more fruit and play sports!

7 – 8 Almost there! Remember to keep clean!

9 – 10 You are in tip-top health! Good job!

😀	🙁
I **go** to school.	I **don't go** to school.
You **go** to school.	You **don't go** to school.
We **go** to school.	We **don't go** to school.
They **go** to school.	They **don't go** to school.
?	
Do you **go** to school?	
Yes, I **do**. / No, I **don't**.	

2 Look and write.

1 I go to school.   🙁 _____ .

2 You brush your teeth.   🙁 _____ .

3 We wake up at seven o'clock.   🙁 _____ .

3 Write questions for a partner. Then ask and answer.

1 <u>Do you play sports?</u> _____

2 _____ ?

3 _____ ?

4 _____ ?

Do you play sports?

Yes, I do.

Language lab 2

SHE EATS / DOESN'T EAT

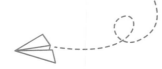

1 Read and chant. Check ☑ or cross ☒ the food below.

1 pizza ☐   2 pears ☐   3 apples ☐

Meet Fozzy, my fruit bat! He likes fruit!
Come and meet him! He's so cool.

Does he eat apples? Yes, he does.
He loves red apples. Yum, yum, yum.

Meet Fozzy, my fruit bat! He likes fruit!
Come and meet him! He's so cool.

Does he eat pears? Yes, he does.
He loves green pears. Yum, yum, yum.

Meet Fozzy, my fruit bat! He likes fruit!
Come and meet him! He's so cool.

Does he eat pizza? No, he doesn't!
He doesn't like pizza. Only fruit!

He **eats** apples every day. 😀

He **doesn't eat** pizza. ☹

Does he **eat** bananas? Yes, he **does**. 😀

Does he **eat** pizza? No, he **doesn't**. ☹

2 Read again. Underline *does* in green and *doesn't* in blue.

3 💡 What's different? Circle.

1 I read my book.
   He reads his book.

2 I brush my teeth every day.
   She brushes her teeth every day.

4 Read and complete.

does   Does   doesn't   eats   he

1 He _____ bananas.

2 He _____ eat pizza every day.

3 _____ he eat apples?

4 Yes, he _____ .

5 No, _____ doesn't.

Language lab 1 and 2

1 Read the blog. Circle the correct words.

I'm Andy. This is my day. I wake up in the morning. I brush my teeth and wash my face. I **1** has / **have** breakfast. I eat fruit and yogurt. Yum! My sister, Ana, doesn't eat yogurt, but she **2** eat / **eats** fruit. I **3** go / **goes** to school with my dad and my sister. After school, I do my homework. I read and **4** write / writes . My dad helps me and my sister, too. We **5** doesn't / **don't** play with our toys. I brush my teeth and go to bed. My dad **6** go / **goes** to bed late.

Is your day busy? When do you **7** wake / wakes up? Write and tell me!

2 Write the questions. Then ask and answer.

1   Andy / eat fruit   Does Andy eat fruit? _____

2   Andy / wake up at seven o'clock?   _____ ?

3   his sister / go to school?   _____ ?

4   Andy and Ana / play with their toys? _____ ?

> Does Andy eat fruit?   Yes, he does.

3 Imagine you are a bat, an owl, or a porcupine! Write about your day.

I am an owl! I sleep in the day.
I don't sleep at night.

_____
_____

3 Lost and found

1  **Watch and circle.**

Anna: My hat is …
- a. green and dirty
- b. green and big
- c. green and soft

2 **Read and complete. Then match. Watch to check.**

mine   yours   Whose

1
_____ hat is this?
It's not _____ !

2
It's not _____ ! It's mine!

3 **Match the person with the object. Then write the name and the object.**

CODE CRACKER

1 _____

2 _____

3 _____

Language lab 1

MINE / YOURS / HIS / HERS

I will ask and answer about objects using **mine / yours / his / hers**.

1 Read the story. Who has a green jacket? Write.

_____

Class 2 go to find their jackets.

"Where are our jackets?" they ask.

"They're here, on the chairs," says Carla.

"Yes, look," says Eva.

"My jacket's green," says Carla. "This jacket's mine. And Juliet has an orange jacket. This is hers. Jake has a yellow jacket. This is his. What color is your jacket, Matthew?"

"My jacket is green," says Matthew.

"Green! The same as mine!" says Carla. "Here's a green jacket. Is it yours?"

"No," says Matthew. "This jacket isn't mine. My jacket has a toy car in the pocket. This jacket has a toy frog in the pocket!"

"Hey! That's mine!" says Carla. "And that's my jacket!"

2 Read and circle T (True) or F (False).

Whose	is it?	
I	My bag is old.	It's **mine**.
You	Your bag is new.	It's **yours**.
She	Her bag is blue.	It's **hers**.
He	His bag is big.	It's **his**.

1   The jackets are on chairs.   T / F

2   Jake has an orange jacket.   T / F

3   There are two green jackets.   T / F

4   There's a toy car in Carla's jacket.   T / F

3 Read again. Underline mine, yours, hers, and his.

4 Read and circle.

1   This pen is (my / mine).

2   Carla has a jacket. It's (her / hers).

3   Joe has a blue ruler. The ruler is (his / he).

4   This is a red airplane. (Who / Whose) is it?

Language lab 2

OUR / OURS   THEIR / THEIRS

I will ask about objects using **ours / theirs**.

1 Read and match.

Jessie:	OK, let's tidy the toys!
Jake:	What's this? It's a very soft teddy!
Jessie:	That's not ours. It's theirs. Here you are.
Tom:	Thanks. Now, our turn.
Tracey:	It's an airplane! That's ours. Let's keep it.
Tom:	Great. Your turn, Jessie and Jake!
Jake:	Thanks. This is interesting. A big, heavy boat! That's ours, Jessie.
Jessie:	Great, I love that boat.
Tom:	What's this? It's strange. It's an old train. Whose is it?
Grandpa:	Hi, kids! What's that?
Jessie:	It's a train.
Grandpa:	That's mine! It's very old. It's special. Thanks, kids!

1 Jessie and Jake ●-   ● a an old train

2 Grandpa ●-   ● b a soft teddy

3 Tom and Tracey ●-   ● c a big, heavy boat

2 Read again. Underline the words whose, ours, and theirs.

3 Read and complete.

1 This is their teddy. It's _____ .

2 Here is our old doll. It's _____ .

3 Here are their jackets. They're _____ .

4 Those are our pens. They're _____ .

Whose is it?

We	It's **ours**. Our bag is small.
They	It's **theirs**. Their bag is purple.

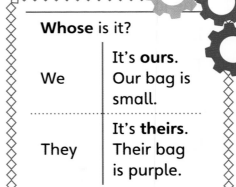

Language lab 1 and 2

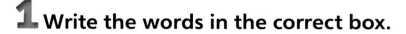

1 Write the words in the correct box.

~~mine~~ ~~my~~ her hers his (2) our ours their theirs your yours

1

That's my pen.

_____

_____

2

That's mine.

_____

_____

2 Complete the dialogs. Then ask and answer.

1 Whose key is this?

It's my key. It's _____ .

2 W_____ airplane is this?

It's his airplane. It's _____ .

3 _____ toy is this?

It's her favorite toy. _____

_____ .

4 _____ box is this?

It's their box. _____

_____ .

5 _____ doll house is this?

It's our doll house. _____

_____ .

6 _____ clock is this?

It's your _____ . _____

_____ .

3 Look and draw. Write sentences. Use his, her/hers, and their/theirs.

bike

jacket

tennis balls

It's his bike.

The bike is his.

_____

_____

_____

_____

17

At the gallery

1 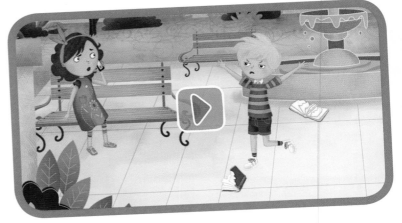 **Watch. Leo is angry. Who is happy? Check ✓.**

☐ Anna ☐ Tom ☐ Milly

2 **Match the questions and answers. Watch to check.**

1 Is this Leo? ●——
2 Is Leo sad? ●——
3 Is Leo tired? ●——

●— a No, he isn't.
●— b No, he isn't tired. He's angry!
●— c No, it isn't.

3 **Look and read. Correct the sentences.**

CODE CRACKER

1 He's angry.   2 She's happy.   3 She's angry.   4 He's funny.

_____ .   _____ .   _____ .   _____ .

Language lab 1

HE / SHE IS / ISN'T

> *I will describe people using **always** / **sometimes** / **never**.*

1 Look and read. Who is never angry?

_____ is never angry.

My soccer friends photo (by Carla)

Here is a photo of my soccer friends! They're great. We're always happy together. Can you see me in the photo? I have dark hair and I'm tall.

Mark's tall, too. He's always helpful. Sue is our captain. She has dark hair like me, but she isn't tall. She's never angry. David's friendly, but he's sometimes naughty. Danny's always kind. He isn't sad, but he's sometimes shy.

And then there is Tom with the ball. He's never lazy. Tom's always funny.

Who are your friends? Do you have a photo of them? Tell me about your friends!

1 Carla

2 _____

3 _____

4 _____

2 Label the people in the photo.

Tom   Mark   Sue

3 Read again. Underline 'm, 're, 's, and isn't.

Is she angry?

Yes, she **is**.

No, she **isn't**. She's fine. She**'s never** angry.

4 Write the questions and answers. Then ask and answer.

Is Carla happy?

Yes, she is.

1 Sue / naughty _____ ?

   ✗ _____ .

2 Tom / lazy _____ ?

   ✗ _____ .

3 Danny / kind _____ ?

   ✓ always _____ . _____ .

Language lab 2

DO YOU HAVE ...?

1 Read and chant. How many animals are in the family? _____

> Do you have a brother? Or maybe even two?
> Oh, let's see … There's Cam and Cody. Yes, I do!
>
> Do you have a baby sister? Is she only one?
> Yes, I do. I have a baby sister. She's a lot of fun!
>
> Do you have a big dog, running in the park?
> Yes, I do. I have a dog. His name is Bark!
>
> Do you have a little cat, running up the trees?
> No, I don't. I don't like cats. Achoo!

Do you have a brother?

Yes, I **do**.

Do you have a sister?

No, I **don't**.

2 Read again. Underline do and don't.

3 Put the words in order.

1   Do   sister?   a   have   you
   Do you have a sister?

2   brother?   a   you   have   Do
   _____

3   do.   I   Yes,
   _____

4   I   No,   don't.
   _____

4 Read and complete.   do   Do   don't   have   you

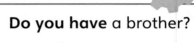

Jasmine: Hi, I'm Jasmine! Nice to meet you.

Bobby: I'm Bobby. Nice to meet you, too. **1** _____ you have a big family?

Jasmine: Yes, I do. I have three sisters!

Bobby: Do you **2** _____ a brother?

Jasmine: Yes, I **3** _____ . I have three brothers!

Bobby: Wow! That is a big family.

Jasmine: What about you? Do **4** _____ have a brother?

Bobby: No, I **5** _____ . I have a pet fish!

Language lab 1 and 2

1 Look and write five sentences. Then ask and answer.

	always	sometimes	never
Tom	friendly	funny	lazy
Anna	kind	shy	naughty
Leo	funny	naughty	shy

I'm **always** kind.

She's **sometimes** lazy.

He's **never** naughty.

Tom is always friendly.

He's sometimes funny.

_____

_____

_____

_____

_____

Is Tom friendly?

Yes, he is. He's always friendly.

2 Look at the photos. Imagine and write sentences.

1 have / sister — I have a sister.

2 sister / Maisie — My sister _____ .

3 Maisie / always / friendly — _____ .

4 Maisie / never / lazy — _____ .

5 don't have / sister — _____ .

6 have / brother — _____ .

7 brother / Kieran — _____ .

8 Kieran / always / funny — _____ .

5 Come in!

1 Watch. What fruit does Leo have in his basket?

a apples and bananas

b apples, oranges, and bananas

c apples, oranges, and pears

2 Read, complete, and then match to the pictures. Watch to check.

 a

 b

 c

1 _____
some pasta, please?

2 _____
some apples, oranges,
and bananas, please?

3 _____
some rice, please?

3 Circle the odd one out.

CODE CRACKER

A apples bananas rice pears

B bread rice pasta oranges

C oranges apple bananas pears

Language lab 1

CAN I HAVE ...?

> I will ask for things politely using **Can I have ... ?**

1 Read and label. What does Daniella eat and drink?

1 _____

2 _____

Waiter:	Good afternoon.
Mom:	Good afternoon. Can I have some pasta and some juice, please?
Waiter:	Yes, you can. And for you?
Daniella:	Can I have some soup and fish, please?
Waiter:	Sure. Anything to drink?
Daniella:	Yes, please. Can I have some water, please?
Waiter:	Yes, of course.

2 Read again. Underline **Can I have.**

Can I have some rice, please?

Sure. / Yes, sure. Here you are. ✓

Mom, **can I have** a candy, please?

Sorry, no. ✗

3 Read the mini dialogs and circle.

1 Can I have some ice cream, please?

Yes, (sorry / sure).

Thanks.

2 Can I have some water, please?

No, (sorry / sure).

Oh, OK.

3 Can I have some bread, please?

Yes, here (you / your) are.

Thanks.

4 Order the words. Write questions.

1 have Can please I pasta some

_____

_____ ?

2 fish please I have Can some

_____

_____ ?

3 please have Can cookie a I

_____

_____ ?

Language lab 2

CAN I HAVE THIS / THAT ...?

*I will ask and answer about objects using **this / that**.*

1 Read. Circle the food at dinner.

a salad and pasta   **b** salad, bread, and pasta   **c** bread and pasta

Aunt: Hello, Mia. Come in. It's dinner time.

Mia: Hello! Oh, great!

Uncle: Do you like pasta?

Mia: Oh yes, Uncle Steven. I love pasta! Mmm ... It's really good. Can I have this salad, please?

Aunt: Here you are.

Mia: Thanks, Aunt Sue. Can I have that strawberry salad, too?

Uncle: Yes, sure Mia.

Can I have this salad, please?

This one? Yes, sure. / No, sorry.

Can I have that salad, please?

That one? Yes, sure. / No, sorry.

2 Read again. Underline this and that.

3 Look and draw lines to match.

1 This   **2** That

4 Look and complete the dialogs.

1

Can I _____ ice cream, please?

Yes, sure.

Thanks

2
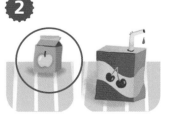

Can I _____ juice, please?

_____ juice?

Yes, please. Thank you.

Language lab 1 and 2

1 Read and complete.

are   have   have some   I   sorry   sure

1   Can I _____ some water, please?
   Yes. Here you _____ .

2   Can I _____ _____ apples, please?
   Yes, _____ .

3   Can _____ have an eraser, please?
   No, _____ . I don't have one.

2  Look and read. Ask and answer.

have some ice cream	✗
have a new toy train	✓
have this mango juice	✗
have a new eraser	✓
have that red airplane	✓

Can I have some ice cream, please?

No, sorry. We don't have ice cream.

3 Look and write questions and answers.

eraser   pencil   water

1   have / some
   _____ ?
   _____ .

2   have / a
   _____ ?
   _____ .

3   have / an
   _____ ?
   _____ .

4 Make a café menu on paper. Give it to a partner. Role-play.

Good afternoon.

Good afternoon. Can I have some apple juice, please?

6 Sports Day

1 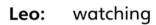 Watch. Check ☑ or cross ☒ the activities.

Leo: watching ☐

Anna: jumping ☐

Leo: kicking ☐

Anna: kicking ☐

2 ▷ Read and match. Watch to check.

1 I •

2 Are •

3 I'm •

4 You •

• a   not running.

• b   'm throwing a ball.

• c   're not watching.

• d   you running?

3 Look and find the activities. Then tell a partner.

I'm running!

CODE CRACKER ⚙⚙⚙

1	t	r	o	r	u	n	n	i	n	g	h
2	c	l	c	l	i	m	b	i	n	g	c
3	w	t	a	w	a	t	c	h	i	n	g	n
4	j	p	g	j	u	m	p	i	n	g	g	j

Language lab 1

I'M JUMPING

> I will talk about actions using **I'm ...ing**.

1 Read. What are they doing? Write one action for each person.

What are you doing today?

Hi, I'm Tad. I live in England. Today I'm playing in the park with my family. It's summer. I'm wearing shorts. I'm not playing basketball today. It's hot. I'm wearing a hat.

Hello. I'm Demi. I live in Canada. Today I'm playing in the snow. I'm not playing soccer in the snow today! It's very cold here. I'm not wearing a T-shirt! I'm wearing a coat.

I'm Jayden. I live in the United States. It's fall. I'm playing basketball with my friends in the park. I'm wearing pants and a sweater. I'm not watching my friends play basketball. I'm playing basketball, so I'm not cold!

I'm **playing** basketball.
You're **wearing** a coat.
Are you **swimming**?
Yes, **I am**.
No, **I'm not**.

I'm = I am
You're = You are

1 Tad   _____
2 Demi   _____
3 Jayden   _____

2 Read again. Underline words that end in -ing.

3 Order the words. Make sentences.

1 playing   are   basketball   You

_____ .

2 not   a   wearing   I'm   coat

_____ .

3 aren't   You   jumping

_____ .

4 watching   not   I'm   soccer

_____ .

Language lab 2

CAN YOU ...?

I will ask and answer about actions using **Can you ... ?**

1 Read. What can you do at Summer Sports Camp?

_____ _____ _____ _____

Summer Sports Camp

Come and try new sports!

Can you swim? Can you run?

Can you play table tennis?

Can you play soccer?

You can't? Don't worry! Come to Summer Sports Camp and learn to do them all!

Can you play table tennis?	
Yes, **I can**.	✓
No, **I can't**.	✗
I can play table tennis.	✓
I can't play table tennis.	✗

2 Look and circle.

1 Can you cook?
   Yes, I can. /
   No, I can't.

2 Can you sing?
   Yes, I can. /
   No, I can't.

3 Can you draw?
   Yes, I can. /
   No, I can't.

3 Write the questions and answers.

1 you / Can / volleyball / play

   _____ ?

   ✓ _____ .

2 Can / jump high / you

   _____ ?

   ✗ _____ .

3 catch a ball / you / Can

   _____ ?

   ✗ _____ .

4 run quickly / Can / you

   _____ ?

   ✓ _____ .

Language lab 1 and 2

1 🗨 **Look at the table. Imagine you are the people. Ask and answer.**

	Jump high	Kick a ball	Play table tennis
Tony	✓	✓	✗
Maria	✗	✓	✓

Hi, Tony. Can you jump high?

Yes, I can.

2 **Read and complete.**

can   can't   'm   wearing   you

Hi Grandpa,

How are you? I'm here at Summer Sports Camp. It's fantastic.
I'm **1** _____ a blue and yellow T-shirt and my favorite blue shorts.
I **2** _____ playing table tennis. I **3** _____ play table tennis now!

It's fun here. The teachers are great. Can **4** _____ still play basketball,
Grandpa? I **5** _____ jump high, but I'm trying!

What are you doing today? Are you in the garden?

See you soon!

Love,

Frankie

3 **Read and answer the questions for you.**

1 What are you wearing? _____ .

2 What are you doing? _____ .

3 Can you play basketball? _____ .

4 Can you swim? _____ .

7 Our home!

1 ▶ Watch. Where is Grandma? Is she cooking?

She is in the _____ .

She is _____ .

2 ▶ Read and complete. Write is or isn't. Watch to check.

1 Leo _____ making a cake.

2 Anna _____ drawing.

3 Dad _____ cooking.

4 Grandpa _____ washing the car.

🇬🇧 British	🇺🇸 American
grandad	grandpa

3 Crack the code! What are they doing?

CODE CRACKER ⚙️⚙️⚙️

1 ● _He is drinking juice._

2 ▲ _____

3 ■ _____

4 ■ _____

Crack the code!

● = he

■ = I

▲ = you

■ = she

Language lab 1

SHE'S COOKING

I will talk about actions using is / isn't ...ing.

1 Read and look. Who is at home?

_____ _____ _____ _____ _____

I'm Gill. It's my dad's birthday today. It's sunny. It isn't raining!

Look at my grandpa. He's in the backyard with my grandma. Is he sitting down? No, he isn't! Grandma's smiling. She isn't cooking, but my grandpa is! Yum – I love barbeques!

Here I am! I'm in the kitchen. I'm making a cake. My friend, Tara, is here, too. She's helping me. Shh, it's a surprise!

Here is my dad. He's sitting in the backyard. He is happy.

2 Read again and underline the sentences with cooking and making.

3 Read again and complete.

1 It isn't _____ .

2 Tara is _____ .

3 Grandma isn't _____ .

4 Gill is _____ .

5 Dad is _____ .

He's **cooking** in the backyard.

She's **helping**.

It's **raining** today.

He **isn't sitting** down.

She **isn't cooking**.

It **isn't snowing**.

🇬🇧 British	🇺🇸 American
barbecue	barbeque

Language lab 2

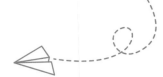

I will ask and answer about actions using **is / isn't ...ing.**

1 Read. What is Sophie doing?

She is _____ .

Mom: Cindy, where is Sophie? We're going to Grandma's house.

Cindy: Oh, I don't know. Let's look. Is she in the living room? Is she watching TV?

Mom: No, she isn't. Hmm … Is she in her bedroom? Is she reading there?

Cindy: No, Mom. She isn't reading in her bedroom.

Mom: Where is she?

Cindy: Hmm … she isn't playing basketball in the yard. Wait! There she is! She has flowers!

Mom: How lovely! She's picking flowers for Grandma. Sophie, the flowers are beautiful. Now, let's go!

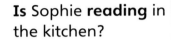

Is Sophie **reading** in the kitchen?

Yes, she **is.** / No, she **isn't.**

Is he **doing** his homework?

Yes, he **is.** / No, he **isn't.**

Is it **raining**?

Yes, it **is.** / No, it **isn't.**

2 Read again. Underline the questions that start with Is.

3 Read and complete. Then write answers.

cleaning   Is   Is he   Is she playing   it

1 _____ she taking a shower?   ✗ _____ .

2 Is he _____ the kitchen?   ✗ _____ .

3 _____ reading in the bedroom?   ✓ _____ .

4 _____ in the yard?   ✓ _____ .

5 Is _____ raining today?   ✗ _____ .

Language lab 1 and 2

1 Look and complete.

> 's   is   is cooking   isn't   isn't   Whose

1 The baby _____ sleeping.

2 Dad _____ dinner.

3 Mom _____ standing.

4 The dog _____ running.

5 Dad _____ friends are here.

6 _____ dog is this? It's Grandma's dog.

Remember!

Whose is it?

It's Tom*'s*.

2 Read the answers. Write the questions.

1 Is my brother _____ ? No, he isn't. He isn't sleeping on the sofa.

2 Is she _____ ? Yes, she is. She is doing her homework.

3 Is Dad _____ ? Yes, he is. He's cooking in the kitchen.

4 Is Dad _____ ? No, he isn't. He isn't sitting on the sofa.

5 _____ ? Yes, it is. It is raining today.

3 Look and complete. Ask and answer with a partner.

	Alice	Dan
teddy bear	✓	✗
hat	✗	✓
box	✓	✗
robot	✓	✗

1 Whose teddy is it? It's _____ teddy.

2 Whose hat is it? _____ hat.

3 _____ ?
_____ box.

4 _____ ?
_____ .

Whose teddy is it? Is it Dan's?

No, it isn't. It's Alice's teddy.

33

1 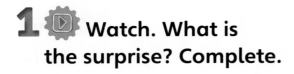 **Watch. What is the surprise? Complete.**

Milly has _____

and _____ now.

2 Complete.

1	___Walk___ →	_Don't walk_
2	Close your eyes. →	Don't close _____ .
3	Turn right. →	Don't _____ .
4	_____ left. →	Don't turn left.
5	Go straight. →	_____ .

3  **You are Anna. Order the instructions. Watch to check.**

CODE CRACKER

a Close your eyes again. ☐

b Walk, walk, now stop! ☐

c Wait. ☐

d Don't open your eyes. ☐ |

e Open your eyes. ☐

f Walk. Go straight. ☐

Language lab 1

WALK / DON'T WALK

I will understand and give instructions.

1 Read and answer. Where are the children?

They are _____ .

Sally: Come on, Rick. Let's go in the kayak together.

Rick: OK. It's fun!

Sally: Wait, Rick! Let me go in.

Rick: Sorry, Sally.

Sally: It's OK. Ready? Go straight.

Rick: Go straight …

Sally: Rick! That's not straight! Stop! Don't turn left!

Rick: Sorry, Sally.

Sally: Just listen to my instructions.

Rick: OK … I'm listening. Sally?

Sally: Er … I'm not sure. Turn left. No, turn right.

Rick: What's wrong?

Sally: I don't know where to go. Mom, can you help?

Stop.

Go straight.

Turn left.

Don't turn left.

2 Read again. Underline Go, Don't, Stop, and Turn.

3 Read and complete. Make rules for Kayak Club.

don't   listen   stop   straight

Kayak Club Rules

1 _____ and wait for your friends.

Don't go quickly.

Go slowly.

Go 2 _____ .

3 _____ hit another kayak.

Always 4 _____ to the instructor.

Language lab 2

ON, IN, UNDER, NEXT TO, BEHIND

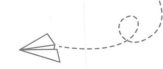

I will use words to describe where things are.

1 Read and answer. How many places are in the chant?

a one   b four   c six

My bag, my bag! It isn't here!
Goldie, can you help me? I'm sure it's near!

Is it in that forest? Or behind this tree?
Good boy, Goldie. Look for it.

Is it under the bridge? Or next to the path?
Good boy, Goldie. Look for it.

My bag, my bag! It's here, it's here!
Good boy, Goldie. Come here.

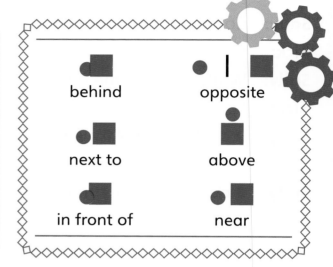

behind   opposite

next to   above

in front of   near

Remember!
in, on, under

2 Read the chant again. Underline the words that say where things are.

3 How many sentences can you make?

| above   behind   in   in front of |
| next to   opposite |

| bird   box   cat |
| garden   river   tree |

The bird is above the tree.

Language lab 1 and 2

1 **Look at the picture. Complete the sentences.**

1 The library is _____ the store.
2 The girl is _____ the movie theater.
3 The café is _____ the museum.
4 The school is _____ the museum.

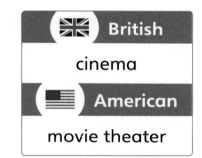

British
cinema

American
movie theater

2 **Imagine and draw a map. Use the places from the list. Give directions to a partner.**

bridge   forest   my house   park   river   school   store

OK. I'm at school. Where is the forest?

Go straight.

Extra Grammar 1

IT'S A ... / ITS HEAD IS ...

I will identify things and belongings with **it's** and **its**.

1 Read and circle.

Is this your cat?

Is this your cat? It isn't mine! It's in our garden. It's lost.

It's cute! It's black.

Its eyes are big and yellow. Its head is small and round.

Is it yours? Call Sandy at

1   Its eyes are blue / yellow .

2   Its head is big / small .

3   It's brown / black .

It's black.   **Its** head is small.

It's cute.   **Its** eyes are big.

It's = It is

2 Read again. Underline *it's* in green and *its* in blue.

3 Circle to complete sentences.

1   **A:** Where is my bag?

    B: It's / Its in the living room.

2   Here is my dog. It's / Its ears are long and soft.

3   It's / Its his pencil case.

4   Here is my favorite doll. It's / Its eyes are green.

4 Write a lost pet poster.

Lost rabbit!

Is this your rabbit?

_____

_____

_____

_____

_____

_____

_____

Extra Grammar 2

I ALWAYS / OFTEN / SOMETIMES / NEVER ...

I will say how often people do activities.

1 **Read the dialog. What sports and activities do Joe and Dan do?**

Joe: _____ _____ _____

Dan: _____ _____ _____

Joe: Hi, Dan. Let's play basketball.

Dan: Hi! Oh, I love basketball! I often play basketball on the weekend. How often do you play?

Joe: I often play basketball with my dad in our yard. I sometimes play table tennis, too. What else do you do in your free time?

Dan: I sometimes play soccer with my sister and I always ride my bike after school.

Joe: Do you like volleyball?

Dan: I never play volleyball. I don't know how to play.

Joe: Really? Maybe I can teach you. I always play volleyball.

Dan: Great, thanks!

> **How often** do you play?
> I **always** ride my bike. ✓✓✓✓✓
> We **often** play basketball. ✓✓✓
> He **sometimes** runs with friends. ✓✓
> They **never** dance. ✗

2 **Read and circle T (True) or F (False).**

1 Joe never plays basketball.   T / F

2 Dan always rides his bike after school.   T / F

3 Joe sometimes plays table tennis.   T / F

4 Dan sometimes plays volleyball.   T / F

3 **Read again. Underline the words that say how often they do something.**

4 Read the text on page 39 again. Check for Joe and Dan. Then check for you.

	Play basketball	Play soccer	Play volleyball	Ride a bike
Joe	_____	We don't know.	_____	We don't know.
Dan	✓ ✓ ✓	_____	_____	_____
Me	_____	_____	_____	_____

5 Put the words in order.

1   do   How   you   often   play soccer

_____?

2   never   I   play music

_____.

3   Tom   with his friends   sometimes   plays in the garden

_____.

4   They   play music   at home   always

_____.

6 Complete the chart for you. Use always, often, sometimes, never.

	Me	
Play the music		
Play table tennis		
Cook dinner at home		
Play soccer		

7 Ask a partner. Complete the chart in 6 for your partner.

How often do you play the piano?

I sometimes play the piano.

Extra Grammar 3

FIRST, GO ... NEXT, TURN / THEN TURN ...

> I will say the order I do things in.

1 Read the dialog. What's next to the library?

The _____ is next to the library.

Ava: Excuse me. Where is the library, please?

James: It's next to the school.

Ava: The new school on West Street?

James: Yes, that's right.

Ava: How do I get to West Street?

James: First, go straight. Go over the bridge. Next, turn left at the park. Then turn right at the museum.

Ava: Ah, I know the museum! Thank you very much.

James: You're welcome!

2 Read again and circle.

1 Ava wants to go to the school / library .

2 The new school is on West Street / East Street .

3 First, Ava needs to go straight / turn left .

4 You turn left / right at the museum.

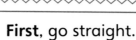
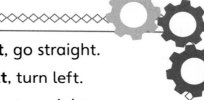

First, go straight.

Next, turn left.

Then turn right.

3 Read again and underline the sentences with first, then, and next.

4 Put the sentences in order.

a Next, turn left. _____

b Then go straight. My house is on the right! _____

c First, turn right. _____

41

5 Read and complete the dialog.

First
is
next
straight
Then

Henry: Hi, Sandra. Let's play a game! I'm at the café.
Where **1** _____ the school?

Sandra: OK. **2** _____ , turn right.

Henry: Turn right, OK.

Sandra: Next, turn left. **3** _____ go **4** _____ .
And the school is on your right. It's **5** _____ to the museum.

Henry: Great, thanks Sandra. Your turn!

6 You are at the café. Write directions to get to the park.
Use First, Next, and Then.

_____

_____

_____

7 Look at the map in 5. Play the game with a partner.

I'm at the school.
Where is the store?

First, turn left …

I will talk about what belongs to other people.

1 Read and underline. What color is Melanie's dress?

Melanie: Oh no! Dad! Look at the living room!

Dad: What is it, Melanie?

Melanie: It is Buddy … And Mom is coming!

Melanie: Oh dear! Buddy, go to the yard. OK, whose green dress is that?

Melanie: It is mine. Thanks. Whose white T-shirt is that?

Dad: It is mine. And this is Mom's blue skirt. Last thing. Is this Tina's gray sweater?

Melanie: Yes, it is. It is her favorite sweater. I can put it back in the bedroom.

Dad: Phew, all tidy now!

Melanie: Hi, Mom! How are you?

Whose skirt is that?

It's Mom **'s** skirt.

2 Read again. Underline the words with 's.

🇬🇧 British	🇺🇸 American
favourite	favorite

3 Whose is it? Look and write.

1   my brother / lizard

_____ .

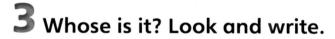

2   Gemma / hat

_____ .

3   my grandma / book

_____ .

Grammar Reference

Unit 1

Language lab 1

Simple Present with *like* (affirmative, negative, and question form):

I *like* cats. I *don't like* frogs.
He *likes* dogs.
She *doesn't like* birds.

Does Tom *like* horses?
Yes, he does. / No, he doesn't.

Language lab 2

There's/There are...

There*'s* a mouse.   There *are* frogs.
There *isn't* a rabbit.   There *aren't* any fish.

Unit 2

Language lab 1

Simple Present for routines and general truths (affirmative, negative, and question form):

I go to the park. *I don't go* to school.
We play soccer. *We don't play* music.
You eat in the café. *You don't eat* in the car.
They go to the shops. *They don't go* to the farm.

On Saturdays, *do you go* to school? No, I don't.
Do you play soccer? Yes, I do.

Language lab 2

Simple Present for routines and general truths (affirmative, negative, and question form):

She eats a banana every day.
He doesn't ride his bike every day.

Does he swim every day?
No, *he doesn't*.

Unit 3

Language lab 1

Possessives: my/mine, your/yours, his/his, her/hers

Whose is it?
It's *mine*. *My* hat is red.

Whose is it?
It's *yours*. *Your* coat is new.

It's *hers*. *Her* bag is heavy.
It's *his*. *His* sweater is dirty.

Language lab 2

Possessives: our/ours, their/theirs

It's *ours*. *Our* ball is green.
It's *theirs*. *Their* book is old.

Unit 4

Language lab 1

***be* verb (third person affirmative, negative, and question form):**

Is he angry?
No, he *isn't*. He*'s* tired.

Is she shy?
Yes, she *is*.

Is she sad?
No, she *isn't*.

Adverbs of frequency: always/sometimes/never

She *is always* shy.
He *is sometimes* tired.
She *is never* naughty.

Language lab 2

***Have* for possession (question form):**

Do you have a lizard?
Yes, *I do*.

Do you have a goat?
No, *I don't*.

Grammar Reference

Unit 5

Language lab 1

Can for permission (question form and natural answers):

Can I have a pear, please?
Sure!

Can I have some building blocks, please?
Sorry, no!

Language lab 2

Can for permission (question form with this/that for proximity):

Can I have *this* book, please?
This one?
Yes!

Can I have *that* ball, please?
That one?
Yes!

Can I have a teddy bear, please?
This one or *that* one?
This one!

Unit 6

Language lab 1

Present Progressive (first person affirmative statements, questions, and short form answers):

I'm eating.

You're sleeping.

Are you drinking water?
Yes, *I am.*

Are you running?
No, *I'm not.*

Language lab 2

Can for ability (question form)

Can you fly?   *Can* you climb trees?
Yes, I *can*.   No, I *can't*.

Unit 7

Language lab 1

Present Progressive (third person singular affirmative and negative statements):

Dad *is cooking* pasta.
He *isn't eating*.
Mom *isn't watching* a movie.
She*'s reading* a book.
The dog *is jumping*.
It *isn't sleeping*.

Language lab 2

Present Progressive (third person singular question and answer forms):

Is he throwing a ball?
Yes, *he is*.

Is she doing homework?
No, *she isn't*.

Possessive 's:

Whose book is it?
It's Mom*'s*.

Whose hat is it?
It's Dad*'s*.

Unit 8

Language lab 1

Imperatives:

Go straight.

Don't go straight.

Turn left.

Don't turn right.

Language lab 2

Prepositions of place:

The ball is *under* the table.
The doll is *next to* the box.
The eraser is *on* the shelf.
The car is *in front of* the ball.
The teddy bear is *in* the box.
The hat is *behind* the box.
The book is *near* the eraser.
The ball is *opposite* the doll.
The train is *above* the eraser.

Pearson Education Limited
KAO TWO
KAO Park
Hockham Way
Harlow, Essex
CM17 9SR
England

and Associated Companies throughout the world.

english.com/englishcode

First published 2021
Second impression 2024

ISBN: 978-1-292-35452-1

Set in Heinemann Roman 13.5

Printed in Slovakia by Neografia

Image Credits:

123RF.com: artinspiring 33, belchonock 43, Cathy Yeulet 19, Daniil Semenov 44, David Franklin 44, Dmitrii Kiselev 27, goodluz 31, joruba 20, Kateryna Davydenko 42, Sergey Novikov 27, szefei 44; **Getty Images:** 7, Bill Oxford 7, Mima Foto 6, 34; **Pearson Education Ltd:** Jon Barlow 26, 29, 33, 35, 42, Rafal Trubisz / Pearson Central Europe SP. Z.O.O: 44, Studio 8 7; **Shutterstock.com:** 31, 44, Andrey N Bannov 28, Andy Dean Photography 44, Anna Photographer 32, 34, 38, Blend Images 32, Cowardlion 44, Dave Montreuil 12, Dean Drobot 43, Diego Cervo 4, Diyana Dimitrova 9, fotosv 15, freedomnaruk 44, Gopfaster 15, iofoto 13, Ivan Kuzmin 13, Jack Jelly 31, Jan Kranendonk 8, Julia Kuznetsova 9, Kapi Ng 41, Karkas 15, Karnizz 9, Kiselev Andrey Valerevich 44, kittirat roekburi 7, Leena Robinson 38, Lopolo 21, Lukas Gojda 3, 6, 12, 18, 21, 32, 34, 37, Merlindo 8, Michael Jung 4, Michael Warwick 7, Mike Orlov 29, molorenz 13, Nate Allred 44, newphotoservice 28, oliveromg 4, pavla 4, Pete Pahham 8, Peter Zvonar 27, Plan-B 7, 31, 37, 43, Ramon Espelt Photography 6, Richard Upshur 4, Robbi 29, Rossario 21, S-F 8, seagames50images 38, Sergei Kolesnikov 7, Sonya Etchison 39, Spotmatik Ltd 24, Teekayu 13, timquo 5, 10, 16, 23, Vladyslav Starozhylov 28, wavebreakmedia 4, 7, Zaikina 36

Animation screen shots

Artwork by Sylvie Poggio, production by Dardanele Studio

All other images © Pearson Education

Every effort has been made to trace the copyright holders and we apologise in advance for any unintentional omissions. We would be pleased to insert the appropriate acknowledgement in any subsequent edition of this publication.

Illustrated by ACA/Sylvie Poggio Artists, pp. 3, 6, 10, 14 (animation characters), 18, 21, 22, 26, 30 (animation characters), 34; Nila Aye/New Division, p. 17; Martyn Cain/Beehive Illustration, pp. 44, 45, 46, 47; Laura Deo/Lemonade Illustration, pp. 16, 24, 25, 30 (drinking, reading, eating); Chiara Fiorentino/ Astound US, p. 37; John Lund/Beehive Illustration, pp. 23, 30 (playing); Mark Ruffle/Beehive Illustration, p. 14 (clock, book, car).

Cover Image: *Front:* **Pearson Education Ltd:** Jon Barlow